Don't Wake the
PRINCESS

HOPES, DREAMS, AND WISHES

Cover Artist
William Joyce writes and illustrates his own
books, such as *A Day with Wilbur Robinson,* and
illustrates books by other authors too. When he
has time, Joyce travels with his wife, Elizabeth,
and his three cats, Boo Boo, Psycho, and Doris
Day.

ISBN 0-673-80041-5

Acknowledgments appear on page 144.

345678910RRS99989796959493

Don't Wake the
PRINCESS

HOPES, DREAMS, AND WISHES

ScottForesman

A Division of HarperCollins*Publishers*

Contents

What Does a Dream Look Like?

What Do Jane Yolen's Characters Want?

AUTHOR STUDY

Animals Dream, Too

GENRE STUDY

LENTIL

BY ROBERT McCLOSKEY

In the town of Alto, Ohio, there lived a boy named Lentil.

Lentil had a happy life except for one thing.
He wanted to sing—but he couldn't!

It was most embarrassing, because when he
opened his mouth to try, only strange sounds
came out. . . . And he couldn't even whistle
because he couldn't pucker his lips.

But he did want to make music, so he saved
up enough pennies to buy a harmonica.

Lentil was proud of his new harmonica and
he decided to become an expert. So he played a
lot, whenever and wherever he could.

A·12

His favorite place to practice was in the
bathtub, because there the tone was improved
one hundred percent.

He used to play almost all the way to school. Down Vine Street to the corner of Main, past the finest house in Alto, which belonged to the great Colonel Carter. Then . . . past the drug store, the barber shop, and the Alto Library, which was a gift of the great Colonel Carter, by the Methodist Church, through the Carter Memorial Park, and around the Soldiers and Sailors Monument that the Colonel had built there.

Then Lentil would stuff his harmonica into his pocket and take a short cut up the alley behind the hardware store so he would not be late for school.

People would smile and wave hello to Lentil
as he walked down the street, because everyone
in Alto liked Lentil's music; that is, everybody
but Old Sneep. Old Sneep didn't like much of
anything or anybody. He just sat on a park bench
and whittled and grumbled.

One day the news got around that the great Colonel Carter, who had been away for two years, was coming home. People began to plan a grand welcome. But when Old Sneep heard the news he said: "Humph! We wuz boys together. He ain't a mite better'n you or me and he needs takin' down a peg or two." Sneep just kept right on whittling, but everybody else kept right on planning. Colonel Carter was the town's most important citizen, so . . .

A·19

the people hung out flags and decorated the streets. The mayor prepared a speech. The Alto Brass Band put on their new uniforms. And the printer, the grocer, the plumber, the minister, the barber, the druggist, the ice man, the school teachers, the housewives and their husbands and their children — yes, the whole town went to the station to welcome Colonel Carter.

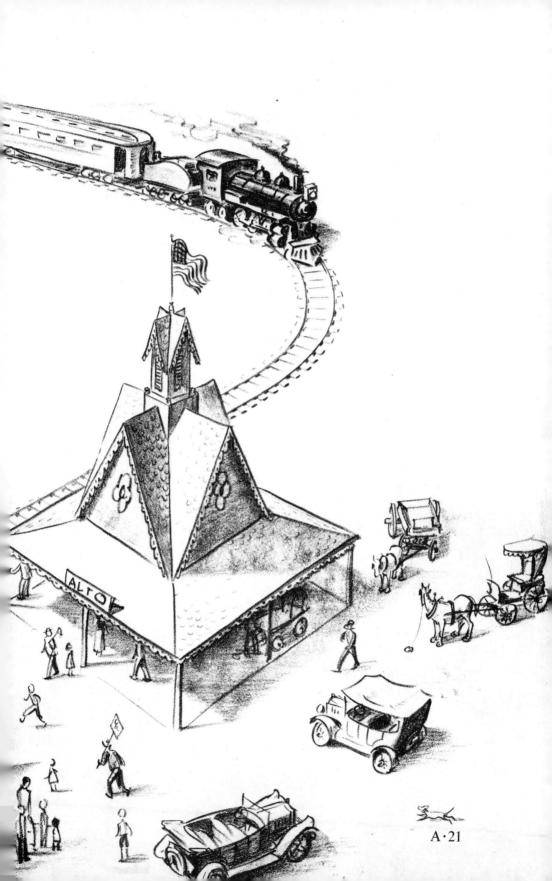

A·21

The train pulled in. The musicians in the band were waiting for the leader to signal them to play. The leader was waiting for the mayor to nod to him to start the band. And the mayor was waiting for Colonel Carter to step from his private car. All the people held their breath and waited. Then there was a wet sound from above. There sat Old Sneep, sucking on a lemon.

Old Sneep knew that when the musicians looked at him their mouths would pucker up so they could not play their horns. The whole band looked up at Old Sneep. The mayor gave the signal to play, but the cornetist couldn't play his cornet, the piccolo player couldn't play his piccolo, the trombone player couldn't play his trombone, and the tuba player couldn't play his tuba, because their lips were all puckered up.

They couldn't play a single note! The musicians just stood there holding their instruments and looking up at Sneep sucking on the lemon. The leader looked helpless. The people were too surprised to move or say a thing. And the mayor wrung his hands and wore a look that said: "Can't somebody do something, please!"

As Colonel Carter stepped from his car, the only sound was the noise of Sneep's lemon.

SHLISH!

Clouds began to gather on the colonel's brow
and he said, "Hmph!" in an indignant sort of
way. Of course Lentil's lips were not puckered
and he knew that something had to be done.
So he took out his harmonica and started to
play "Comin' 'Round the Mountain When
She Comes."

When Lentil began to play the second chorus,
Colonel Carter smiled.

Then he let out a loud chuckle and began to sing,
"Driving Six White Horses When She Comes."

A·27

Then everybody sang and they all marched
down Main Street behind the colonel's car.

Lentil rode with the colonel, who took a turn
at the harmonica when Lentil's wind began to
give out. (He said that he hadn't played one since
he was a boy, but he did very well considering.)

They marched to the colonel's house and paraded through the gate and onto the front lawn. The mayor's committee served ice cream cones to all the citizens and Colonel Carter made a speech saying how happy he was about such a fine welcome and how happy he was to be home again. When he said that he was going to build a new hospital for the town of Alto, everybody was happy—even Old Sneep!

So, you never can tell what will happen when you learn to play the harmonica.

THINKING ABOUT IT

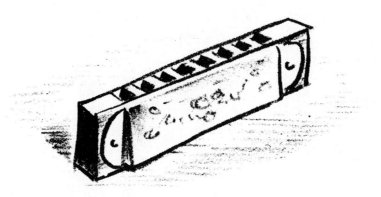

1. Lentil saved the day by playing his harmonica for the colonel. Tell about a time when you had a really bright idea that helped solve a problem.

2. Have you ever seen a bathtub with claws? Do you carry your books tied with a belt? Look at the pictures. What clues do you find that show this story takes place in the past?

3. Colonel Carter wants to give the town something. He's thinking of giving a statue, a flag, or something else in honor of Lentil. What would you suggest? Why?

Another Book by Robert McCloskey

Read about Homer Price and his wacky adventures with the odd characters in small-town America in *Homer Price*.

Builders, 1980

A·32

JACOB LAWRENCE

Painter of the American Scene

by Kathleen Stevens

How far would you walk to learn about something that interested you? When he was young, Jacob Lawrence often walked more than sixty blocks from his home in the Harlem section of New York City to the Metropolitan Museum of Art. Jacob wanted to be an artist, and he believed that studying the famous paintings hanging in that museum would help him.

The year was 1930. The depression had brought hard times. Many people were out of work, and money was tight. The families who lived in Harlem suffered greatly

Strike, 1949

from the depression, but still the streets were filled with energy and color.

As he walked through Harlem, Jacob noticed the people on the stoops and sidewalks. He looked hard at the churches and pool halls, the funeral parlors and barbershops. Jacob stored those images in his mind, along with the images of paintings he saw in the museum.

Jacob came from a poor family. His mother believed there was little chance that her son could grow up to be a successful painter. She wanted him to aim for something more practical. But Jacob's teacher in an after-school art program saw that the youngster was talented. Charles Alston showed him how to use poster paints and crayons to make papier-mâché masks and cardboard stage sets.

As time passed, Alston let Jacob rent work space in his own studio. That studio was an exciting place for a young black man struggling to become an artist. Many creative people gathered there to talk about art and literature and history.

From these conversations, Jacob learned that history books often ignored the accomplishments of African Americans. He decided to paint a series of pictures dramatizing the story of a black hero. He chose Toussaint L'Ouverture, a slave from the Caribbean island of Haiti, who had helped free his people from French rule.

Many people admired Lawrence's pictures, but he needed more than admiration. To help his family, he often had to work at jobs that took him away from painting. Then something encouraging happened. The government set up the Federal Art Project to help struggling artists survive the depression, and a sculptor named Augusta Savage got Lawrence a job with the project.

The Migration of the Negro, Panel No. 1, 1940–41.

A·37

Harriet Tubman Series, No. 7, 1939–40

For eighteen months, Lawrence was paid a salary to paint pictures. For the first time, he felt like a professional artist.

During his participation in the project, Lawrence painted two more series, using Frederick Douglass and Harriet Tubman as his subjects. Frederick Douglass was an ex-slave who became a famous writer and a powerful antislavery speaker. Harriet Tubman escaped from slavery herself, then returned to the South to lead other slaves to freedom. In his powerful paintings Lawrence made the stories of these brave people come alive.

In a third series, *The Migration of the Negro,* Lawrence painted pictures that showed how thousands of African Americans left farms in the South during World War I to look for jobs in northern cities. *Fortune* magazine printed twenty-six of those pictures in 1941, the first time a national magazine had devoted so much space to an African American artist.

That same year Lawrence married Gwendolyn Knight. On their honeymoon in New Orleans, Lawrence received exciting news. A New York art gallery wanted to represent his paintings. Until then, no African American artist had ever been offered the chance to sell his work regularly through a major gallery.

Back home in New York, Lawrence created a new series of Harlem paintings. In these paintings he put the busy streets, cold-water apartments, and crowded nightclubs he remembered from his youth.

When the U.S. entered World War II, Lawrence was drafted into the Coast Guard, where he continued painting as a Coast Guard artist. His ship was the first U.S. military vessel that combined blacks and whites as crew members. Lawrence said later that the USS *Sea Cloud* gave him the best experience of democracy he had ever known.

Lawrence returned home to find that his paintings were winning prizes and attention from the critics. He was invited to illustrate books and also to teach at

Black Mountain College in North Carolina. All that success put pressure on Lawrence. Realizing that he needed help, Lawrence entered a mental hospital.

During his eight months of treatment, Lawrence produced a series of paintings showing what it was like to be mentally ill in a hospital ward. Lawrence learned much about himself during this time. He was again ready to move forward as a painter.

In the years since, Lawrence has led an interesting life. He has taught in art schools and universities, and his work has received many honors. He has traveled as far as Nigeria.

In 1971 Lawrence moved with his wife to the Northwest so he could accept a teaching position at the University of Washington. They have lived in Seattle ever since.

During these years of travel and teaching, Jacob Lawrence has been painting steadily, producing easel paintings, posters, murals, and illustrations for books. Most of his subjects spring from the American scene.

Because he finds libraries so helpful when he does research, Lawrence has painted pictures set in libraries. Because he admires builders and their tools, he has painted many pictures of workers. Our society has changed since Lawrence was a child. Now people of all colors, men and women, work side by side. Lawrence's paintings show them that way.

When he was young, Jacob Lawrence stood in front of the paintings on the walls of the Metropolitan Museum and dreamed of becoming an artist. Today, he is one of the most famous artists in the country. His own paintings hang in many museums—including the Metropolitan.

THINKING ABOUT IT

Tools, 1978

1. Jacob Lawrence is visiting your town to find ideas for some new paintings. From what you know about the artist, what parts of your town would you show him? Why?

2. What parts of Jacob Lawrence's life do you think helped him become an artist? Why?

3. Jacob Lawrence worked and studied to become good at painting. What advice would you give a friend who wants to become really good at something—for example, telling stories or playing soccer?

The River That Gave Gifts

Written and Illustrated by
Margo Humphrey

IN A HOUSE on the side of a country meadow, there lived a girl named Yanava. She was a beautiful dark brown child who found it difficult to make things with her hands.

But she thought about many things, and what her hands could not create, her mind could.

Her nearby friends were Oronde, Kengee, and Jey. They had played together all their lives, and they had one special thing in common: they all loved Neema, the wise old woman of the

town, who had always listened to them and
answered their questions.

The children knew that Neema loved colors
because of the fine quilts that she made. They
also knew that her eyes were growing dim. So
they decided they would each give her something
that showed their love before the time came
when she would not be able to see.

Jey looked through the colorful buttons in her old button jar and found some that her grandmother had given her. They were worn with age and all golden on the edges like the setting sun. Jey chose the loveliest buttons of all and strung them on a chain for Neema.

Kengee made ribbon bows from the bits and pieces of bright cloth that she found in her mother's sewing box. She cut and put them together just so, for Kengee cared very much for Neema.

Oronde built a box to hold all of Neema's precious things. He carefully chose each piece of wood. He fitted the pieces together and made a handle so that the box would be easy for Neema

to carry. Then he polished the box until it shone with all the love he had put into making it.

While Jey, Kengee, and Oronde were working on their gifts, Yanava went to her favorite place to think about what she could give Neema.

She sat down beside the river which flowed through her yard. "What should the present be?" she asked herself. "Should it be large or small?" And most importantly, "What does Neema need the most?"

It was quiet and peaceful. The river sparkled ever so brightly from the sun. It was as if someone had thrown diamonds upon the water as it flowed by.

Soon the river began to whisper, "Take me into your hands. Take me into your hands." The murmur of the river began to send her into a peaceful sleep.

The river was old and wise with the wisdom of the ancient ones. The river knew the gift that Yanava should give to Neema, the elder.

As Yanava slept, the river murmured over and over, "Take me into your hands. Take me into your hands."

When Yanava awoke it was nighttime, and she knew that the river had given her the answer. She knelt at the water's edge to refresh herself after her nap. As she washed her hands, she began to see rays of light fly off her fingers.

"Can this be?" she said. The harder she rubbed, the brighter the light became.

The river whispered, "You, Yanava, beautiful black child, have the gift of light. Let me show you. Hold out your hands."

A·47

She held out her hands, and the light streaming from her fingers changed into different colors.

From her thumbs came the color red, the color of happiness. From her first fingers came the color yellow, the color of the sun which is the soul of all living things. From her second fingers came the color green, the color of life. From her third fingers came the color blue, the color of birth and water. And from her little fingers came the color violet, the color of royalty.

The day finally arrived for the presentation of Neema's gifts.

First to enter the dimly lighted room was Oronde, who presented the box he had made. It was a beautiful box, but Neema could barely see it. "Thank you," she said.

Next came Kengee with her ribbon bows woven together into a colorful piece to hang on the wall. Then came Jey with her old buttons strung on an elegant chain. But it was difficult for Neema to see these gifts in the dim light of the room.

At last came Yanava, who had waited patiently while the others presented their gifts. She kissed Neema on the forehead and asked politely, "Now may I present my gift?" Neema nodded.

Yanava reached into her bag and took out a jar of river water. Carefully, she removed the lid and poured the water into her hands as the ancient river had told her to do. Then she rubbed her hands together, and the light rays began to form just as they had by the river's edge.

Yanava stood with her hands extended as the colors of the rainbow flowed from her fingers. The dark room was transformed into a vision of color, and Neema could see. *Neema could see!*

Now Neema could see all of her presents because of Yanava's special gift—the gift of light.

Thinking About It

1. The four children have just given you the gifts they gave to Neema in *The River That Gave Gifts*. What will you do with each of the gifts?

2. If you were the river, how would you help people? Why?

3. Think of a person who is as special to you as Neema is to Yanava. What gift would you like to make for this special person? Why is your gift a good one for that person?

We Could Be Friends

by Myra Cohn Livingston

We could be friends
Like friends are supposed to be.
You, picking up the telephone
Calling me

    to come over and play
    or take a walk,
    finding a place
    to sit and talk.

Or just goof around
Like friends do,
Me, picking up the telephone
Calling you.

A·52

What If

by Beatrice Schenk de Regniers

What if
my cat
could talk
and give me good advice
(but only when I asked for it)!
Wouldn't that be nice?

What if
my goldfish
learned by heart
forty-five or fifty
lullabies to sing to me!
Wouldn't that be nifty?

What if
my dog
were smart
and taught me how to spell
and helped me with my homework!
Wouldn't that be swell?

What if
my cat,
my dog,
my goldfish
all arranged to meet
and celebrate my birthday!
Wouldn't that be *sweet?*

A·53

The Flame of Peace

A TALE OF THE AZTECS

DEBORAH NOURSE LATTIMORE

Once a great, long time ago, the capital of the Valley of Mexico had another name. It was called Tenochtitlán, Land of the Aztecs. Bustling marketplaces brimmed with people. Merchants traded in the sunny plazas. In gleaming temples priests made offerings. And even though we do not know as much as we would like about the Aztecs, we do know about their art, their gods, their wars, and their hopes for peace.

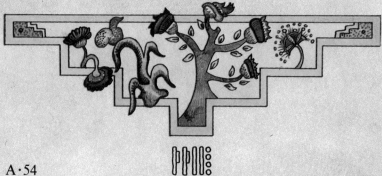

There was once a boy called Two Flint, who
fished in the sparkling lake outside the city walls.
Two Flint knew of no better place on earth.

One day, Two Flint saw battle flags fluttering
on the towers. Warriors stood along the walls.
Emperor Itzcoatl himself appeared before the

temple, draped in his imperial robes.

"Tezozomoc and his army are in the hills," the Emperor said. "He plans to capture our city. We must prepare ourselves. We will send ambassadors with gifts. Then we will see what kind of enemies these men are."

Five Eagle, Two Flint's father, went to the marketplace to count the gifts for Tezozomoc.

"Why do we send gifts to our enemies?" asked Two Flint.

"For the Twenty Days of Talking," answered Five Eagle. "We will show Tezozomoc how great we are by sending him our best things."

"Will there be peace after the Twenty Days?" asked Two Flint.

"Maybe peace. Maybe war," his father said. "Who knows? We have been enemies for many years."

The next morning Five Eagle stood in front of the temple with the other ambassadors. Priestesses danced before the stairs as smoke curled up from incense burners. Conch shells sounded from tower to tower. The Emperor raised his arms. The ambassadors saluted him.

"One day you may have to search for peace, Two Flint," said his father. "Be brave when that day comes!" Then he marched from the city.

For twenty days and twenty nights, Two Flint climbed the towers and squinted at the road leading to the hills. At last, ragged and limping figures appeared, but the father of Two Flint was not among them. Tezozomoc's warriors had taken his life.

"Let us prepare for war," said the Emperor.
"Tezozomoc has broken the Twenty Days of
Talking." He spilled copal juice down his face
and right arm. "Tomorrow we face our enemy!"

Later, at home, Two Flint and his mother,
One Flower, talked sadly.

"Did we always fight the people from the

shores of Lake Texcoco?'' Two Flint asked.

"Oh, no," she said. "Once the sacred light of the Morning Star burned in our temples and we were all brothers. But now the fire is dying. With no New Fire from Lord Morning Star, there can be no peace, only war."

"Where is Lord Morning Star?" asked Two Flint.

"There is a long road beyond the great city walls ruled by nine evil demons of darkness. At the end of the road is the Hill of the Star. That is where they say Lord Morning Star can be found. But all who have ever searched for him were soon lost." His mother shook her head.

The night, like a burning obsidian bowl, glowed with the flickering torches of foot runners as the city prepared for war. Temple altars blazed with fiery offerings of incense. Conch shells and bone whistles sang from the towers. At the House of Singing, warriors drank their favorite maize porridge, perhaps for the last time. Some sang while others danced a dance of war.

"If the New Fire burned in the great temple," Two Flint thought, "we would have peace. Tomorrow I will find Lord Morning Star and tell him we need his light!"

Two Flint's mind was made up. As he slept, he dreamed that the summer skies whirled their clouds around the moon. Lord Morning Star burst through the circle of moonlight. He spoke to Two Flint.

"Fight the nine evil ones, Two Flint," Lord Morning Star said. "But use your wits, not your

sword! I wait for you! Come! Come!''

The next morning, the mighty Aztec army,
weapons shining in the dazzling sunlight,
marched away on the road to the hills. On the
long mountain road, a single Aztec boy set off for
the Hill of the Star.

"Two Flint!" called One Flower. "Why are
you leaving?"

"My father told me to be brave and to search for peace," he answered.

"Then," One Flower said, "you must go."

The pale maize sun of dawn was hot amber when Two Flint came to the crossroads, where the first evil demon awaited him.

"Go back!" growled a voice. "I am Crossroads, and no one passes me!"

"Mighty Lord Crossroads," said Two Flint, "I seek one greater than you!" Two Flint crossed his arms over his chest and stood tall.

"Greater than I?" said Crossroads. "I, who can change the path of River?" His arms whipped up and down, faster and faster until the banks of River shook.

"Lord River! Greater than Lord Crossroads!" called Two Flint, running to the riverbank. "Wash away all but the true road!"

"I am greater than Crossroads," gurgled Lord River. He dove deep into the riverbed and filled his mouth with water. Suddenly a giant waterspout swept away Lord Crossroads.

Two Flint jumped past River, but water was filling the road.

"Great Lord Wind!" called Two Flint, his heart beating wildly. "Mightier than Lord River! Blow Lord River back!"

"Wind always blows stronger than River's current!" a howling, airy voice whistled. Over Two Flint's head a gust of wind blew, in torrents, in streams, in mighty bursts, pushing River back into his bed.

Two Flint climbed the steep riverbank, but

Lord Wind blew him down.

"You fooled Crossroads and River," howled Lord Wind, "but you can't fool me!"

"Perhaps I am not powerful enough to fool you, mighty Wind," called Two Flint, "but look! Lord Storm has passed by you!" And he pointed ahead on the road to huge, gloomy, black clouds.

Lord Wind turned dark blue as he puffed up his cheeks and blew a giant gale. But Storm's frogs opened their mouths. Hail and rain flew like arrows across the sky, and the frogs swallowed Lord Wind.

Two Flint's legs shook and wobbled as he scrambled up the road. Lord Storm passed behind. The ground ahead crumbled and cracked.

"Go back! No one passes Earthquake!" rumbled a voice below.

Two Flint grabbed the trunk of an old, gnarly tree.

"If you are so powerful, why is Lord Volcano taller than you?" Two Flint yelled.

The voice grumbled. Two Flint pressed himself tightly against the tree. Lord Earthquake roared and shook. The ground rippled through the tree's roots and split the bark.

"Lord Volcano!" Two Flint shouted. "Let Lord Earthquake shake the ground to pieces! You can put them back together!"

Smoke and ash filled the air. Lord Volcano poured out his fire and the rocks melted together.

"You passed ahead of Storm and you escaped Earthquake," bellowed Lord Volcano, "but you can't fool me!" Down poured his rocky fire.

Two Flint climbed from the tree to a cave
high on a cliff. He held his breath as fiery rocks
tumbled everywhere. When Lord Volcano
stopped, the entrance was blocked. Two Flint
was trapped.

Suddenly a cool wisp of air trickled over Two
Flint's feet. He caught it in his fingers and
followed it to another opening.

"Go no farther!" thundered a voice outside. "I am Lord Smoking Mirror, the great trickster, and no one passes me without first holding my cloak!" A shadow larger than the sky darkened the road.

Two Flint knew that of all Lord Smoking Mirror's tricks, his cloak of forgetfulness was the most powerful. Quickly, Two Flint gathered together a pile of rocks and made a statue of himself. He pushed it out the opening. Down swooped the demon and dropped his cloak over the statue and flew away. Two Flint had tricked him.

His heart pounding hard and loud, Two Flint ran up the road until he came to a thick mist filled with the sounds of gnashing teeth and clattering bones. Out sprang the Lord and Lady of Death.

"Approach, Spirit! Now you belong to us!" they hissed, shaking their bones.

"Step back!" shouted Two Flint. "I am still alive! I fooled seven lords. You have power over the dead. But you have no power over me!" Faster than the jaguar, he shot up a steep hill and bolted through the clouds.

Spicy incense and flowers perfumed the air. Billowy clouds sparkled brighter than all the Emperor's jewels. Two Flint was on the top of the Hill of the Star.

"You have struggled long and hard, Two Flint," said a deep, calm voice. High over the mist appeared Lord Morning Star, bathed in silvery rays of moonlight. Glistening gold flames encircled him.

"In your search for peace, fighting with only your wits, you have found me. You are the new One of Peace, Prince Two Flint. Take the New Fire!'' A brilliant flame on a feathery torch tumbled down to Two Flint.

Two Flint found himself running on the road toward Tenochtitlán, the New Fire glimmering in his hands. Behind him Lord Morning Star shone, spreading rays of red and gold across the sky.

All along the walls, warriors who had fought their way into the city threw down their weapons and greeted Two Flint. Emperor Itzcoatl himself welcomed Two Flint as he climbed the stairs of the great temple and placed the New Fire on the altar.

"Let all fighting end!'' Two Flint announced. "From this day on, let our city be a brother to all cities!''

That evening the people sang and danced. Itzcoatl's warriors and Tezozomoc's warriors broke their spears and embraced as friends.

Deep inside the temple, the glow of a single fire burned bright and true.

We know that the Aztecs feared nine evil lords of darkness and believed in a god of peace. Could a boy have outwitted those evil lords and struck a New Fire of peace from the Morning Star? All we know is that during the time of Itzcoatl, a great Alliance of Cities marked the beginning of many peaceful decades.

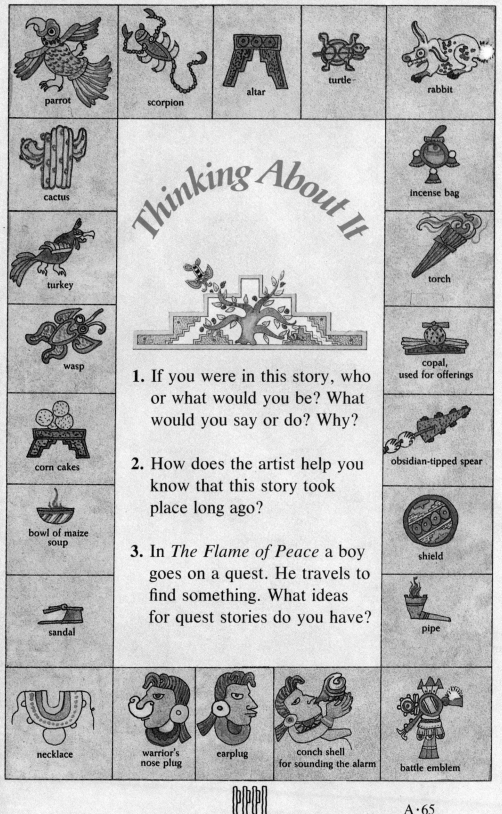

parrot

scorpion

altar

turtle

rabbit

cactus

turkey

wasp

corn cakes

bowl of maize soup

sandal

incense bag

torch

copal, used for offerings

obsidian-tipped spear

shield

pipe

necklace

warrior's nose plug

earplug

conch shell for sounding the alarm

battle emblem

Thinking About It

1. If you were in this story, who or what would you be? What would you say or do? Why?

2. How does the artist help you know that this story took place long ago?

3. In *The Flame of Peace* a boy goes on a quest. He travels to find something. What ideas for quest stories do you have?

OWL MOON

by Jane Yolen
illustrated by John Schoenherr

It was late one winter night,
long past my bedtime,
when Pa and I went owling.
There was no wind.
The trees stood still
as giant statues.
And the moon was so bright
the sky seemed to shine.
Somewhere behind us
a train whistle blew,
long and low,
like a sad, sad song.

I could hear it
through the woolen cap
Pa had pulled down
over my ears.
A farm dog answered
   the train,
and then a second dog
joined in.
They sang out,
trains and dogs,
for a real long time.
And when their voices
faded away
it was as quiet as a dream.
We walked on toward
   the woods,
Pa and I.

Our feet crunched
over the crisp snow
and little gray footprints
followed us.

Pa made a long shadow,
but mine was short
   and round.
I had to run after him
every now and then
to keep up,
and my short, round shadow
bumped after me.

But I never called out.
If you go owling
you have to be quiet,
that's what Pa always says.

I had been waiting
to go owling with Pa
for a long, long time.

A·69

We reached the line
of pine trees,
black and pointy
against the sky,
and Pa held up his hand.
I stopped right where I was
and waited.
He looked up,
as if searching the stars,
as if reading a map up there.
The moon made his face
into a silver mask.
Then he called:
"Whoo-whoo-who-who-who-whooooooo,"
the sound of a Great Horned Owl.
"Whoo-whoo-who-who-who-whooooooo."

Again he called out.
And then again.
After each call
he was silent
and for a moment we
  both listened.
But there was no answer.
Pa shrugged
and I shrugged.
I was not disappointed.
My brothers all said
sometimes there's an owl
and sometimes there isn't.

We walked on.
I could feel the cold,
as if someone's icy hand
was palm-down on my back.
And my nose
and the tops of my cheeks
felt cold and hot
at the same time.
But I never said a word.
If you go owling
you have to be quiet
and make your own heat.

We went into the woods.
The shadows
were the blackest things
I had ever seen.
They stained the white snow.
My mouth felt furry,
for the scarf over it
was wet and warm.
I didn't ask
what kinds of things
hide behind black trees
in the middle of the night.
When you go owling
you have to be brave.

A·73

Then we came to a clearing
in the dark woods.
The moon was high above us.
It seemed to fit
exactly
over the center of the clearing
and the snow below it
was whiter than the milk
in a cereal bowl.

A·75

A·76

I sighed
and Pa held up his hand
at the sound.
I put my mittens
over the scarf
over my mouth
and listened hard.
And then Pa called:
"Whoo-whoo-who-who-who-
whooooooo.
Whoo-whoo-who-who-who-
whooooooo."
I listened
and looked so hard
my ears hurt
and my eyes got cloudy
with the cold.
Pa raised his face
to call out again,
but before he could
open his mouth
an echo
came threading its way
through the trees.
"Whoo-whoo-who-who-who-
whooooooo."

Pa almost smiled.
Then he called back:
"Whoo-whoo-who-who-who-
whooooooo,"
just as if he
and the owl
were talking about supper
or about the woods
or the moon
or the cold.
I took my mitten
off the scarf
off my mouth,
and I almost smiled, too.

The owl's call came closer,
from high up in the trees
on the edge of the meadow.
Nothing in the meadow
  moved.
All of a sudden
an owl shadow,
part of the big tree shadow,
lifted off
and flew right over us.
We watched silently
with heat in our mouths,
the heat of all those words
we had not spoken.
The shadow hooted again.

Pa turned on
his big flashlight
and caught the owl
just as it was landing
on a branch.

For one minute,
three minutes,
maybe even a hundred minutes,
we stared at one another.

Then the owl
pumped its great wings
and lifted off the branch
like a shadow
without sound.
It flew back into the forest.
"Time to go home,"
Pa said to me.
I knew then I could talk,
I could even laugh out loud.
But I was a shadow
as we walked home.

When you go owling
you don't need words
or warm
or anything but hope.
That's what Pa says.
The kind of hope
that flies
on silent wings
under a shining
Owl Moon.

Bird Watcher

by Jane Yolen

Across the earless
face of the moon
a stretch of Vs
honks homeward.
From the lake
laughs the last joke
of a solitary loon.
Winter silences us all.
I will miss
these conversations,
the trips at dawn
and dusk,
where I listen carefully
then answer
only with my eyes.

Thinking About It

1. The child in *Owl Moon* shares an unforgettable experience with her father on a cold, snowy night. If you had been along, what would you have remembered best?

2. Trees stand like giant statues. Trains and dogs sing out in the night. Snow is "whiter than milk in a cereal bowl." Jane Yolen uses words like these to give a picture of walking in a snowy woods late at night. Pick out a few of your favorite phrases from *Owl Moon*. Share them with others in your class.

3. Describe an exciting experience you'd like to have in your life—an experience that would make a good picture book. With whom would you share it?

A·84

JANE YOLEN

SLEEPING UGLY

illustrations by
DIANE STANLEY

rincess Miserella was
a beautiful princess if you counted her eyes and
nose and mouth and all the way down to her
toes. But inside, where it was hard to see she
was the meanest, wickedest, and most worthless
princess around. She liked stepping on dogs. She
kicked kittens. She threw pies in the cook's face.
And she never—not even once—said thank you
or please. And besides, she told lies.

In that very same kingdom, in the middle of the woods, lived a poor orphan named Plain Jane. She certainly was. Her hair was short and

turned down. Her nose was long and turned up. And even if they had been the other way 'round, she would not have been a great beauty. But she loved animals, and she was always kind to strange old ladies.

One day Princess Miserella rode out of the palace in a huff. (A huff is not a kind of carriage. It is a kind of temper tantrum. Her usual kind.) She rode and rode and rode, looking beautiful as always, even with her hair in tangles.

She rode right into the middle of the woods and was soon lost. She got off her horse and slapped it sharply for losing the way. The horse said nothing, but ran right back home. It had known the way back all the time, but it was not about to tell Miserella. So there was the

princess, lost in a dark wood. It made her look even prettier.

Suddenly, Princess Miserella tripped over a little old lady asleep under a tree. Now little old ladies who sleep under trees deep in a dark wood are almost always fairies in disguise. Miserella guessed who the little old lady was, but she did not care. She kicked the old lady on the bottoms of her feet. *"Get up and take me home,"* said the princess.

So the old lady got to her feet very slowly — for the bottoms now hurt. She took Miserella by the hand. (She used only her thumb and second finger to hold Miserella's hand. Fairies know quite a bit about *that* kind of princess.)

They walked and walked even deeper into the wood. There they found a little house. It was Plain Jane's house. It was dreary. The floors sank. The walls stank. The roof leaked even on sunny days.

But Jane made the best of it. She planted roses around the door. And little animals and birds made their home with her. (That may be why the floors sank and the walls stank, but no one complained.)

"This is not *my* home," said Miserella with a sniff.

"Nor mine," said the fairy.

They walked in without knocking, and there was Jane. "It is mine," she said.

The princess looked at Jane, down and up, up and down. "Take me home," said Miserella, "and as a reward I will make you my maid."

Plain Jane smiled a thin little smile. It did not improve her looks or the princess's mood. "Some reward," said the fairy to herself. Out loud she said, "If you could take *both* of us home, I could probably squeeze out a wish or two."

"Make it three," said Miserella to the fairy, "and *I'll* get us home."

Plain Jane smiled again. The birds began to sing. "My home is your home," said Jane.

"I like your manners," said the fairy. "And for that good thought, I'll give three wishes to *you*."

Princess Miserella was not pleased. She stamped her foot. "Do that again," said the fairy, taking a pine wand from her pocket, "and I'll turn your foot to stone." Just to be mean, Miserella stamped her foot again. It turned to stone.

Plain Jane sighed. "My first wish is that you change her foot back."

The fairy made a face. "I like your manners, but not your taste," she said to Jane. "Still, a wish is a wish." The fairy moved the wand. The princess shook her foot. It was no longer made of stone.

"Guess my foot fell asleep for a moment," said Miserella. She really liked to lie. "Besides," the princess said, "that was a stupid way to waste a wish."

The fairy was angry. "Do not call someone stupid unless you have been properly introduced," she said, "or are a member of the family."

"*Stupid, stupid, stupid,*" said Miserella. She hated to be told what to do.

"Say stupid again," warned the fairy, holding up her wand, "and I will make toads come out of your mouth."

"*Stupid!*" shouted Miserella. As she said it, a great big toad dropped out of her mouth.

"Cute," said Jane, picking up the toad, "and I *do* like toads, but . . ."

"But?" asked the fairy. Miserella did not open her mouth. Toads were among her least favorite animals.

"But," said Plain Jane, "my second wish is that you get rid of the mouth toads."

"She's lucky it wasn't mouth elephants," mumbled the fairy. She waved the pine wand. Miserella opened her mouth slowly. Nothing came out but her tongue. She pointed it at the fairy.

Princess Miserella looked miserable. That made her look beautiful, too. "I definitely have had enough," she said. "I want to go home." She grabbed Plain Jane's arm.

"Gently, gently," said the old fairy, shaking her head. "If you are not gentle with magic, none of us will go anywhere."

"You can go where you want," said Miserella, "but there is only one place I want to go."

"*To sleep!*" said the fairy, who was now much too mad to remember to be gentle. She waved her wand so hard she hit the wall of Jane's house.

The wall broke. The wand broke. The spell broke. And before Jane could make her third wish, all three of them were asleep.

It was one of those famous hundred-year-naps that need a prince and a kiss to end them. So they slept and slept in the cottage in the wood. They slept through three and a half wars, one plague, six new kings, the invention of the sewing machine, and the discovery of a new continent. The cottage was deep in the woods so very few princes passed by. And none of the ones who did even tried the door.

At the end of one hundred years a prince named Jojo (who was the youngest son of a youngest son and so had no gold or jewels or property to speak of) came into the woods. It began to rain, so he stepped into the cottage over the broken wall.

He saw three women asleep with spiderwebs holding them to the floor. One of them was a beautiful princess.

Being the kind of young man who read fairy

tales, Jojo knew just what to do. But because he was the youngest son of a youngest son, with no gold or jewels or property to speak of, he had never kissed anyone before, except his mother, which didn't count, and his father, who had a beard.

Jojo thought he should practice before he tried kissing the princess. (He also wondered if she would like marrying a prince with no property or gold or jewels to speak of. Jojo knew with princesses that sort of thing really matters.) So he puckered up his lips and kissed the old fairy on the nose. It was quite pleasant. She smelled slightly of cinnamon.

He moved on to Jane. He puckered up his lips and kissed her on the mouth. It was delightful. She smelled of wild flowers. He moved on to the beautiful princess. Just then the fairy and Plain Jane woke up. Prince Jojo's kisses had worked. The fairy picked up the pieces of her wand.

Jane looked at the prince and remembered the kiss as if it were a dream. "I wish he loved me," she said softly to herself.

"Good wish!" said the fairy to herself. She waved the two pieces of wand gently. The prince looked at Miserella, who was having a bad dream and enjoying it. Even frowning she was beautiful.

But Jojo knew that kind of princess. He had three cousins just like her. Pretty on the outside. Ugly within.

He remembered the smell of wild flowers and turned back to Jane. "I love *you*." he said. "What's your name?"

So they lived happily ever after in Jane's cottage. The prince fixed the roof and the wall and built a house next door for the old fairy.

They used the sleeping princess as a conversation piece when friends came to visit. Or sometimes they stood her up (still fast asleep) in the hallway and let her hold coats and hats. But they never let anyone kiss her awake, not even their children, who numbered three.

Moral: Let sleeping princesses lie or lying princesses sleep, whichever seems wisest.

WHY I WROTE
SLEEPING UGLY

by Jane Yolen

W hen I was growing
up, I loved to read folk tales and fairy tales. I
read all of the Andrew Lang color fairy books—
*The Blue Fairy Book, The Orange Fairy Book,
The Green Fairy Book,* and all the rest. I adored
the stories and became each of the heroines in
turn: the girl on the back of the white bear in
"East of the Sun, West of the Moon," the
Hoodie-crow's daughter, the farmer's wife stolen

away by the fairies. Funny thing, though, almost all of the heroines were small boned and slender, golden haired and sweet.

When I looked in the mirror, I was dark haired and dark skinned and chunky. If I had any cheekbones, they were well hidden behind the cheeks. And even though I took years of ballet, I had large flat feet and a center of gravity that— to be kind—was centered rather lower in my anatomy than the girls who danced the cygnets in ''Swan Lake.'' People who loved me said I was cute. Perky. Funny. Smart. All I heard was the under-message: I was plain. Plain Jane.

Now to be honest, there are very few absolutely gorgeous women in the world. Most of us, the great majority, ninety-nine percent of us, are cute. Perky. Funny. Smart. One or another of these. And plain.

That's why I wrote *Sleeping Ugly,* in part. So that the plain but good-hearted, perky, funny, smart girl could win the prince. So the sassy old fairy (I am now a sassy old lady!) could get the good lines. And so the prince would—for once—make the right choice and not be blinded by the heroine's beauty.

And, because, I like to make people laugh. When they read *Sleeping Ugly,* they do!

THINKING ABOUT IT

1. As you read this story, who did you root for?
Did you want Miserella to wake up? Did you
want Jane to marry the prince? Tell why.

2. If you read or performed parts of this story on
TV, which parts would you choose? How
would you do them?

3. What would happen in the story if Miserella
woke up? What other stories does this one
remind you of? Why?

Another Book by Jane Yolen

In *The Girl Who Loved the Wind,* a father
tries to protect his daughter from all
unhappiness by hiding her from the world. But
when the wind whispers the truth into her ear,
something unexpected happens.

Tucker Mouse Finds a Friend

from *Harry Kitten and Tucker Mouse*

by George Selden
Illustrations by Garth Williams

At least I could have a name!" the tiny mouse said to himself.

He was picking his way, very carefully, along the gutter of Tenth Avenue in New York City. *Whssht!*—just like that, he'd dart from under one parked car to the dark dirty safety beneath another. For this young little mouse had found that the human beings didn't like him much. Some of those two-legged creatures, who thought they owned the whole city, called him a rat—which he definitely was *not!*—when they saw him. And some called him a rodent. And one just said, "Yeck!"—which sounded most unkind of all.

"But at least I can have a name," the mouse said, as he paused to nibble the crust of a cheese sandwich that one of the human beings had thrown away. He wished there had been more cheese and less crust. "My own name." He quickly hid behind a tire, as a threatening leather boot came near.

"I could be Hamlet. Hamlet Mouse." The night before, in the theater district, the young mouse had heard two human beings, very well dressed, say that they were going to a show called *Hamlet*. "But I don't like 'Hamlet,'" the mouse said to himself. "It sounds too much like a little pig."

There was another possibility. Godzilla Mouse. Two teenage boys were going to a horror movie and the mouse had overheard them talking. "Godzilla Mouse—?"

"It just isn't me," he decided.

But who was he? If he didn't have a name, he

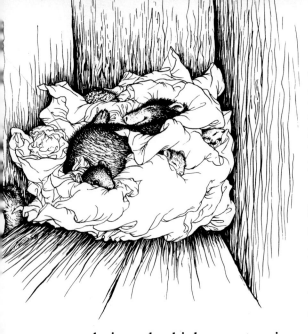

wouldn't be anyone. For a name makes a person very special. He is *himself*—and no one else.

A group of young girls walked by the car under which the mouse was hiding.

These laughing young girls—one of them had soft fuzzy hair and a high sweet voice—reminded the mouse of the very first thing that he could remember. That was a nest, made of scraps of cloth, and thrown-away Kleenexes, and other comfortable, cozy odds and ends. And there also was a soft warm furry weight—the word "Mother" rang in his ears—that tried to protect him from pounding shovels, and nasty words, and the threat of death. There were men in uniforms, sanitation workers. And he ran.

He'd run, the young mouse had, and *still* was running.

Since then, there'd been no warmth, no weight, no comforting covering. There had only been darting from one parked car—a temporary refuge—to another.

"But I have to have a *name!*" the mouse said. "So even if I do get tromped on—at least I'll know who's being squashed!"

The motor of the car he was under started up with a roar. The mouse jumped aside.

His jump landed him very near those girls. And in order not to frighten them, because young girls and young mice sometimes do not get along, he hid between two garbage cans. Not a very nice place, to be sure—but the little mouse had been in worse. And also, he was near enough to hear the girls talking, a rippling, happy sound.

"I'm hungry," said one.

"So'm I," said another.

"Well, this is the best bakery on Tenth Avenue," said a third girl. "Merry Tucker's Home-Baked Goods. Does anyone feel like a glazed doughnut or a raspberry tart? They're to *die* over, they're so good!"

The girls twittered their excitement. And went into the bakery.

And oh!—a glazed doughnut! A raspberry tart! The little mouse—whose mouth was now watering—could have died over either one. But something even more interesting echoed in his ears. *Merry Tucker's Home-Baked Goods.*

He felt there was something special in those words. A name!

"It can't be Merry," he said to himself. "Sounds too much like Mary." And if you were going to grow up and be a "he" mouse—well, a name like Mary would just not do.

But Tucker—he mused and repeated the name. "Tucker Mouse." It sounded quite original. Not ordinary like Tom, or Joe, or Bill. "*Tucker* Mouse!" he shouted. "That's me."

The name tasted more sweet and more strong in his mouth than even a raspberry tart.

So, armed with his name, the mouse
marched—through the gutter, it's true—but he
marched down Tenth Avenue. His name—Tucker
Mouse—which he'd looked for so long gave him
strength, courage—gave him life!

Tucker Mouse skittered after the girls, darting
close to the buildings that lined the street. He
was hoping that one of the girls might drop a
little piece of pastry. But, sadly, they all liked
tarts and doughnuts as much as he did, and
smacking their lips, which made it worse, not one
of them dropped a single crumb.

Then up ahead he saw what he feared most of
all in the world: a garbage truck—and all around
it, sanitation workers scooping up trash from the
sidewalk. Tucker Mouse knew that the uniformed
men thought he was trash too. He felt lonely and
afraid again.

And tired. So tired. He had to find a place to
rest. A narrow, dark alley opened between a
tenement and a dry cleaner's. As Tucker was
scooting in, he happened to see a small copper
coin on the sidewalk. Instinctively, he snatched it
up in his two front paws—then vanished into the
sheltering dark.

"A penny!" he exclaimed out loud—quite
proud that he'd found it, and saved it.

"The human beings think pennies are good
luck," said a voice behind him.

Tucker whirled around. In the dark behind
him, nibbling a crust—the remains of a
sandwich—he saw a kitten. His first thought was:
Poor guy! He's as starved as I am. But then

he remembered: I am a *mouse*—and this is a
kitten, who will very likely become a *cat*.

"Ya wanna fight?" he demanded.

"Why?" The kitten put down his crust, and
simply asked, "Why?"

"Well—well—" Tucker Mouse was flustered.
"It's just that—well—cats and mice *fight*.
That's all."

"But why?" the kitten continued to question.
"I was starving to death before I found this
pitiful piece of sandwich. Some overfed human
being missed that garbage can, so *I* got to eat.

And you don't look too beefy yourself. So why make life worse for each other by fighting?"

Tucker Mouse was somewhat taken aback. He hadn't expected such reasonable talk from a skinny kitten sitting next to a trash can and a decaying pumpkin.

"But what do we do if we *don't* fight?" asked Tucker.

"Mmm—" The kitten purred softly, like a philosopher. "We could just be friends—"

"*What—?*"

"Not so loud. The human beings are all around."

Tucker nodded ruefully: they were surrounded.

"I know that it's unusual," said the kitten. "At least, I know it's supposed to be. But this is New York! And all the rules are broken here. For the best, I hope. We might even set a precedent—"

"What's a precedent?"

"It's a new way of thinking," said the kitten. "And a new way of feeling too."

"You promise not to eat me?"

"I will never be *that* hungry." The kitten patted the small mouse's head. "And even if I was—I couldn't. My teeth aren't big enough. Yet."

"Mmm—" The mouse had to think about that. "For a mouse to trust a cat—"

"You've got to trust somebody—sooner or later," the kitten declared. "Why not try me?"

"Well—okay. For a while. But I'm keeping an eye on those teeth!"

Tucker sighed and looked down the alley, where some sanitation workers were doing their job. For a moment he even wished them well. They have problems, too, he thought to himself— but I hope that I am not one of them.

"You want some sandwich?"

Tucker Mouse said nothing.

"Come on," urged the kitten. "It's ham-and-cheese. Mice like cheese—"

"Ohhh!" Tucker groaned with delight.

"Then just you munch on this piece. See? There is ham and *also* cheese on this crust."

"I *am* sort of hungry—" admitted Tucker. "But it isn't a raspberry tart."

"Well, listen to the mousiekins!" The kitten purred. "Next time I'll try to supply—"

"Don't you *dare* call me mousiekins!"

"—beef steak. Or corned beef."

"Oh, can I have a bite?" said the mouse. "I'm so *hungry!* You can't believe—"

"It's all yours," said the kitten. "I'm full."

"Full?" The thought of being full of food had never occurred to the mouse before.

"Munch out!" said the kitten.

And Tucker munched.

Between mouthfuls—for there's more to a crust than a human being might think—he asked, "What's your name?"

And then, before the kitten could answer, he explained, between munches, why his name was Tucker.

"Why, that's very much like—it's exactly what happened to me!" said the kitten. And friendship, like a frail tree, grew between them.

Thinking About It

1. You are standing on the corner of a busy street and you see Tucker Mouse, hungry and lonely, hiding beneath a parked car. How will you help him?

2. If you told this story to a friend as if you saw it happen, what things would your friend find difficult or impossible to believe? Why?

3. Plan your own animal fantasy. What animals will you use as characters? Give your characters names, and tell what happens to them.

Another Book by George Selden
Tucker and his kitten pal make another new friend in *The Cricket in Times Square*.

THE DOG
That Pitched a No-Hitter

by Matt Christopher

The day was hot and muggy, the field was soggy from last night's rain, and Mike didn't feel well. What pitcher would, Mike thought, if he were put into a game in the fifth inning, and his team were trailing by nine runs?

The Lake Avenue Bearcats were beating the Grand Avenue Giants by a score of 19 to 10.

Why do we even have to finish this lousy game? Mike thought. The Bearcats will just pile up more runs against us, that's all.

" 'Cause it's the rules, pal," he heard a voice in his head say. "And you ought to know you can't bend the rules, right?"

Mike glanced over to the Giants' bench and saw Harry, his Airedale, relaxing in the shade. "Right," Mike answered him in his thoughts.

Mike and Harry shared a very special secret: they could communicate with each other through ESP, extrasensory perception. Mike had seen the Airedale in the window of a pet shop one day and was surprised to discover that he could understand the dog's thoughts, and the dog could understand his! Of course, Mike bought Harry right away, and that was the start of one of the best friendships ever between a kid and a dog.

"This batter's easy," Harry was telling him now. "Keep them down by his knees. He's a sucker for low ones."

"Sure," Mike answered. "If I had good control, I'd try it."

Mike got on the mound, stretched, and threw a pitch. The baseball streaked toward the plate—belt high.

POW! The batter socked it high and deep to center field.

"No sweat," Mike heard Harry say. "Frankie'll catch it in his back pocket."

Frankie Tuttle, the center fielder, had to run back just a few feet. Maybe he would have been able to catch it in his back pocket if he had tried. But he used his glove instead.

Mike breathed a sigh of relief. One out. Five more to go—two this inning, three the next.

The Bearcats' next batter came to the plate.

"Bugsy O'Toole, Mike," Harry said. "As dangerous as he looks too."

"I know, I know," said Mike. "He's already got a homer and a triple. Shall I walk him?"

"Keep them low and inside," Harry advised.

Mike aimed at the low inside corner of the plate and for once managed to throw the ball exactly where he wanted it to go. Bugsy O'Toole swung at it, drove a hot grounder to third base, and Jerry Moon threw him out.

"There you go," said Harry.

Mike smiled. "Thanks, pal," he said.

Harry liked to watch the other teams practice before the games so he could learn the players' strengths and weaknesses. He had a keen eye, but what was really remarkable about him was his memory.

Wish I could remember the way he does, Mike thought.

The next Bearcat hit a high infield fly. Jim Button, the shortstop, caught it, and the top half of the sixth inning was over.

Mike was relieved for a while, but then the Giants couldn't get a man on base at their turn at bat. Mike was back on the mound before he knew it. He tried hard, but even with the help of Harry's coaching, he allowed two hits, and a man scored. At the top of the seventh, it was Bearcats 20, Giants 10.

The Giants failed to score when they batted for the last time, and the game went to the Bearcats.

"I shouldn't have let that run score," Mike said with frustration as he and Harry headed for home.

"You tried your best. Give yourself some credit," Harry said. "You sure were better than that first pitcher."

Mike shrugged. "I hope the coach doesn't decide to have me start against those Peach Street Mudders on Friday. They're no easy pickin's, either."

"I know," said Harry. "They're numero duo."

Mike looked at him. "Numero what?"

Harry grinned. You could always tell he was

grinning by the way his mouth curved up at the corners and the way he lifted his wiry eyebrows.

"Number two," he said. "I've been learning a lot by watching educational television. Like this, for instance."

Harry stopped and did something Mike had never seen him do before: a dance. A crazy dance, on two legs.

"What is *that?*" Mike asked, wide-eyed and laughing.

"You like it?" said Harry. "It's the Bunny Hop."

"You crazy dog! You'd better stop that before some cop picks you up and hikes you to the dog pound!"

"Yeah, right." Harry stopped his crazy dance. "From what I've heard about dog pounds, they're not for an intelligent, capable creature like me."

Mike shook his head. "Harry," he said, "I don't know what to do with you. But I don't know what I'd do without you, either!"

Harry grinned again. Then he hopped up into Mike's arms and licked his face.

The next four days were difficult for Mike. He worried more about pitching against the Peach Street Mudders than he did about any homework or test his teachers could give him. He'd rather write any report—no matter how long—than pitch against the Mudders.

The Mudders had played four games so far and won them all. Most of the players were big guys who could hit a ball a country mile. They were players like Barry McGee, who averaged a home run a game, and Turtleneck Jones, who was almost as big and tough as Barry.

"I don't want to think about them," Mike said to himself, while playing catch with his father in the backyard. "Maybe I'll be lucky. Maybe Coach Wilson will have somebody else pitch."

"Pal, you're worrying too much about nothing," said Harry, who was resting comfortably under the shade of a nearby tree. "Relax. Old buddy Harry will tell you what to do. I'll practically pitch the game for you."

"Oh, sure," Mike thought back to Harry, as he caught his father's soft throw. "The great Harry the Airedale. Dog pitcher. Strikes out McGee with the bases loaded. You're out of your mind, Harry."

"Control, man," said Harry. "All you need is control. I'll tell you what to pitch to each guy as he comes to the plate, and you take it from there."

"That'll be fine, except that I don't have control," Mike grumbled. "All I've got is speed."

"Did you say something, son?" his father asked.

Mike shook his head. "Sorry, Dad," he said. "I was talking to myself."

Sometimes Mike forgot to communicate mentally with Harry and started talking out loud. Mike and Harry had made a pact that nobody—not even Mike's parents—would find out their secret, but sometimes that made for embarrassing moments.

At last came the day of the game against the Peach Street Mudders. And, as Mike had feared, Coach Wilson had him pitch.

The Mudders were first up at bat, and Mike was scared from the start. He walked the first batter and hit the second batter on the foot, putting him on base too. Then tall, dark-haired Barry McGee strode up to the plate.

"Pitch high and outside to him," said Harry, who by now was pacing back and forth in the Giants' dugout. "That's his weak spot. I watched him during batting practice."

"I'll try," said Mike.

But once again he was too nervous to follow Harry's instructions. He stretched, and pitched. The ball went straight over the heart of the plate. Barry knocked it to center field, where Sparrow Fisher caught it . . . then dropped it!

"Oh, no!" Mike groaned, as he watched two runs score and Barry go safely to second base.

"Have faith, pal," Harry said. "Have faith."

"That's easy for *you* to say," Mike said.

Nobody else scored that inning nor the next. In the third, the Giants got three men on—one on a walk, one on a passed ball by the pitcher, and one on an error, a sizzling grounder through the third baseman's legs.

Monk Solomon, the Giants' first baseman and only slugger on the team, drilled the first pitch through the pitcher's box to center field. The ball struck something in front of the fielder and bounced over his shoulder to the fence. By the time the fielder picked it up and threw it in, all three runners—and Monk—scored.

The Giants' fans went crazy.

It was Grand Avenue Giants, 4; Peach Street Mudders, 2.

The score stayed that way until the top of the seventh inning, when Mike, nervous as a mouse trapped in a room full of cats, hit the first batter on the shoulder, walked the second, and fumbled the third man's bunt.

"Oh, no!" Mike groaned again. "No outs, and three men on! What'll I do now, Harry?"

A hit could tie the score. A *long* one could put the Mudders ahead. Mike's heart pounded.

"Harry?"

No answer.

Mike looked over to the dugout where he had last seen Harry. But there was no Harry.

Sweat glistened on Mike's face. "Harry!" his mind screamed. "Where are you? I need your moral support . . . now!"

Still no answer.

"Play ball!" cried the ump.

Mike got on the mound. Just then the fans began to laugh.

Mike was flustered. What was so funny? He tried to concentrate on aiming his pitch, but he couldn't remember what the batter usually went for. As the ball left his hand, he knew it was headed right toward the middle of the plate. He braced himself for the hit that was sure to come.

"Strike!" yelled the ump, to Mike's surprise. The batter must have been distracted too.

Mike sped another across the plate. "Strike two!"

And another. "Strike three!"

The fans kept roaring with laughter as the next batter—who was trying hard not to laugh too—stepped up to the plate.

They must be laughing at me, Mike thought. First I fill up the bases, then I get my first strikeout. That *is* something to laugh about.

He struck out the second batter too.

And the fans kept laughing.

Let 'em laugh, Mike thought to himself. For the first time since the game had started, Mike began to relax.

Then the next batter walked up to the plate. It was Turtleneck Jones. He wasn't laughing. He looked angry and determined.

But Turtleneck tried too hard.

"Strike one!" the ump called, as Turtleneck swung at Mike's first pitch and missed it by a mile.

"Strike two!" the ump said, as Turtleneck chopped the air a second time.

Then, "Strike three!" the ump yelled, as Turtleneck swished for the third time.

"You did it! You did it!" Monk cried, running to Mike from first base. "You pitched a no-hitter!"

Mike's eyebrows arched. "I did *what?*"

He didn't even realize the game was over until he saw the crowd leaving the grandstand and the fans running toward him, cheering and laughing.

"Nice game, Mike," said Coach Wilson, as he shook Mike's hand. "But I think you got a little help from that dog of yours."

Mike stared at the outfield, where Coach Wilson was pointing. There, doing a crazy, twisting dance on the platform in front of the scoreboard, was Harry.

"Oh, no!" Mike cried. "Is that what the crowd was laughing at?"

"The crowd, and some of the batters too," said the coach. "I think you owe that dog a few extra dog biscuits tonight, Mike."

Mike grinned. "I sure do!"

Seconds later, Harry came sprinting across the baseball field toward him.

"Harry!" Mike cried as the dog sprang into his arms. "What the heck were you doing?"

"The Bunny Hop, remember?" said Harry. "Want to see me do it again?"

He jumped to the ground and started kicking out his legs.

"I think you've danced enough for one day," said Mike, laughing.

When he pulled himself together, he went on, "Why did you leave me alone out there, anyway?"

"I never left you," said Harry. "I just thought we needed a different strategy. I took some of the pressure off by entertaining the crowd a little."

"Isn't that cheating?"

Harry turned serious. "No way! You pulled your own weight all along. I saw you stand up to Turtleneck Jones."

Mike remembered how relaxed and in control he had felt. "I guess you're right," he admitted.

"Of course I'm right," Harry said. "All you needed was some confidence."

"And a dog who thought he was a rabbit!" Mike said, grinning.

"Naturally," said Harry, who Bunny Hopped all the way home.

A·120

WRITING
THE DOG
That Pitched a No-Hitter

Matt Christopher

by Matt Christopher

Books that make you laugh are not the easiest books in the world to write. But I thought that a dog and a boy who could read each other's minds would be humorous and unusual characters. If I mixed these characters with a popular sport, I believed I'd have a terrific combination for a book. So I came up with Harry, an Airedale, and his master Mike and their secret—the ability to communicate with each other by ESP.

I wanted an eye-catching title and one that would give the reader an idea what the book was about. I decided on *The Dog That Pitched a No-Hitter*.

I dreamed up the theme for the book next. What was my book going to be about? It would be about a boy, Mike, who is worried that his pitching for his team, the Grand Avenue Giants, wouldn't succeed against the Peach Street Mudders, a team with some of the league's best hitters.

I wrote up lists of the players on the teams and their positions, and wrote down important scenes. Then I wrote an outline of my book in a few paragraphs. This is a must when you write a book. You must know where your book is going before you write the first word.

Then, with my plot outline beside me, I wrote the book, double spaced, on my word processor. Because it's Mike's story, I wrote it from his viewpoint all the way through.

When I was finished writing, I set aside the manuscript for a couple of weeks. Then I went back to it and checked and rechecked the scenes and the spelling. I worked on the manuscript until I felt confident it was the best it could possibly be.

Then, and not before then, I put the manuscript in a large envelope and mailed it with a letter to my publisher.

I hope you like it!

Thinking About It

1. You are Mike. You've just lost the game with the Bearcats. What will you do to prepare for the next tough game against the Mudders?

2. You could say that Harry is Mike's coach. What does Harry do and say that reminds you of a coach?

3. Borrow Harry for a day. What task will you give him to do? Why?

Another Book by Matt Christopher
Is Harry a thief? Find out in *The Dog That Stole Football Plays,* in which Harry switches his talents to the football field.

CHARACTERS

TURTLE   FARMER

PIGEON 1   BOY

PIGEON 2   WIFE

PROP LIST

(These things can be real or mimed.)

HAND PROPS

feathers that can be pulled off Pigeons and
     stuck onto Turtle, rope, corn

*(The mood of this play is soft, lyrical, and
whimsical. It might be established with the
sound of orchestra bells, water glasses,
xylophone, marimba, or flute. The
instrument you choose could then be used
to accompany* TURTLE's *singing.)*

NARRATOR: There was once a turtle who was
a dreamer. He couldn't run very fast. And he
couldn't swim very far. He couldn't dance
very well. But he could sing just beautifully.
*(*TURTLE *enters singing a la-de-da tune
without words.)*

NARRATOR: And because he could sing
very well, he would sing for hours every
day. Sometimes he would sing about things
he liked.
*(*TURTLE *sings to himself a little song without
words that deals with things he likes.)*

NARRATOR: And sometimes he would sing about things he didn't like.

(TURTLE *sings a little wordless song about hateful things.*)

NARRATOR: But mostly he would sing about things he wished he could do.

TURTLE: *(while singing, he attempts to do these actions).*

I wish I could swim like a wiley green
   crocodile.

I wish I could run like a lovely gazelle.

I wish I could swing from my tail like
   a monkey.

And, if I try hard enough,

And, if I try hard enough,

And, if I try hard enough,
   you never can tell,
   you never can tell,

If I try hard enough,
   perhaps I could do it!

NARRATOR: But what he really wanted to do more than anything else was to fly.

(PIGEONS *fly in a circle around the stage. Actors can make up any movement they wish for the flying.* TURTLE *stops singing and watches them in awe.*)

TURTLE: Oh, I wish I could fly. I wish I could fly more than anything else in the world. If I could take up flying, I'd even give up singing. Yes, gladly.

(PIGEONS *fly by again.*)

TURTLE: Birds! Say, Pigeons! Please come here. I want to talk to you, but I can't go that fast.

PIGEON 1: Hello, there, Turtle. *(landing)*.

PIGEON 2: *(landing)*. Hello, friend. We thought we heard you singing as we flew by.

PIGEON 1: It sounded lovely. It makes me feel like flying.

PIGEON 2: Would you mind singing another little tune right now? I'd like to try it out.

TURTLE: Yes, I'll sing a verse or two. *(He sings his little tune.)*
(PIGEONS are taken over by the song and dance-fly until TURTLE stops singing.)

PIGEON 1: *(landing beside TURTLE)*. That was marvelous.

PIGEON 2: *(landing)*. When you sing, it makes me feel like dancing-flying.

TURTLE: Oh, thank you. It makes me feel like flying too. In fact I always feel like flying. But I can't. I've tried and tried, but I absolutely can't do it. Would you watch me? Maybe you can tell what I'm doing wrong.
(PIGEONS watch while TURTLE makes a very concentrated and clumsy attempt to move his flippers and feet; his shell restricts him severely.)

PIGEON 1: You are trying hard enough . . .

PIGEON 2: . . . But it will never work. If you ask me, it's because you have no feathers.

PIGEON 1: Feathers! Why, last year, when I molted and lost all my feathers . . .

PIGEON 2:   . . . you couldn't fly a bit.

PIGEON 1:   Right. I had to wait till they'd all grown in again.

TURTLE: Feathers! I've never had any feathers. I don't think I'll ever grow any either, because I've been waiting to fly for a long time and not a single feather has grown.

PIGEON 2:   Look, I'll give you a few of mine. I don't need *every* last one.

PIGEON 1:   I can spare some too. I'd like to help you out with this because I certainly do appreciate your singing for us.
(PIGEONS *take feathers from their wings and stick them in the* TURTLE's *shell.*)

TURTLE: (*growing more and more excited as each feather is added.*) I'm beautiful! Oh, look, how beautiful I am!
(*He spins around to display feathers.*)
I feel all dressed up with no place to go. Where shall we fly?

PIGEON 1:   We were just on our way to the corn field over there next to you. Come along with us, and we'll have a corn feast to celebrate.
(PIGEONS *fly to the far side of stage, and* TURTLE *follows clumsily, but too excited to notice his "flying" doesn't work very well.*)

TURTLE: This is wonderful. I am flying! I am just like one of the pigeons.

PIGEON 1:   The corn is much better than it was last week.

PIGEON 2:   It's not bad. Fuller kernels. (*To* TURTLE.) Are you enjoying it, friend?

A·128

TURTLE: Oh . . . yes, delicious experience. *(He tries to eat with the rest of them but is too excited.)*

PIGEON 1: I was afraid it would never ripen.

PIGEON 2: Well, there wasn't enough sun for it until this week.

PIGEON 1: True. *(To* TURTLE.*)* Say, don't eat the husk. The good part's inside.

TURTLE: *(in confused manner).* Yes, of course. I'm getting to it now.

PIGEON 1: *(moving to a new place for more corn, notices something offstage).* Quick! Fly. The farmer's coming.

PIGEON 2: *(darting over to look).* His boy is with him, too. Get out fast.

PIGEON 1: They killed two crows last week. Hurry up. *(The* PIGEONS *fly around the* TURTLE *with great alarm.* PIGEON 1 *exits one way.)*

PIGEON 2: Come on! Fly. Fly. *(Exits another way.)*

TURTLE: I'm coming. Don't wait. I can't fly as fast as you can yet. I'll catch up in a minute. *(*TURTLE *tries to fly, flapping his flippers fiercely. He covers no ground.* FARMER *and* BOY *enter, see him;* FARMER *signals to* BOY *to grab* TURTLE. FARMER *is overly authoritative in his commands, and the* BOY *is so full of fun and the silliness of things that the* FARMER's *commands don't get through to him.)*

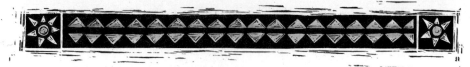

FARMER: Get him.

(They do a slapstick mix-up here with BOY *grabbing* FARMER, *who then throws him off. Each grabs for a flipper, but* TURTLE *quickly pulls flippers into his shell.* FARMER *finally seizes* TURTLE *by neck.)*

FARMER: I've got him. Go get a rope.

BOY: Rope? *(Playing with the sounds of the word.)* Rope, rope, rope . . .

FARMER: The rope!

(BOY dashes off to get it.)

We can have stewed turtle with our corn tonight.

(BOY dashes back on immediately with rope.)

TURTLE: I'm not a turtle. I'm a bird.

FARMER: You look like a turtle to me.

(They put rope around his neck.)

TURTLE: Well, I'm a flying turtle.

BOY: Then, why didn't you fly?

TURTLE: *(hurt by the truth).* Oh . . .

(FARMER and BOY start to walk home with the TURTLE between them.)

NARRATOR: Yes, the turtle was disappointed. But he realized this was no time for wishful thinking, so he said to himself:

TURTLE: Under the circumstances, I think I'd better give up flying and take up singing. *(TURTLE starts to sing and FARMER and BOY, overcome by the sound, begin to sway and dance, increasing their movements until they completely entangle themselves and the TURTLE with rope. TURTLE stops singing.)*

FARMER: Now, look what you've done!

BOY: It wasn't my fault. You were dancing too.

FARMER: Never mind about that. Get me untangled.

(BOY makes it worse.)

No, the other way.

(They get straightened out.)

I'll take the turtle home; you get the corn.

BOY: Corn?

(*Again playing with the sounds of the word.*)
Corn, corn, corn . . .

FARMER: Go get the corn!

BOY: Corn! (*Dashes out and falls down before disappearing, offstage.*)

(FARMER *starts to walk home with* TURTLE *on rope.* BOY *appears again and mischievously slaps out a rhythm on his leg.*)

FARMER: The corn! (BOY *scrambles out again.*)

(FARMER *continues walk home.* WIFE *comes out to establish the house.*)

FARMER: Wife, here is a surprise for you. We caught a delicious turtle for supper. Start to cook him . . .

TURTLE: Oh! (*Shrinks into shell.* FARMER *and* WIFE *look with surprise.*)

FARMER: . . . while I go help our boy get the corn.

WIFE: Gladly. This is a treat. He'll be ready to eat by the time you get back.

(FARMER *leaves and* WIFE *prepares to go to work. Looks* TURTLE *over carefully, becoming puzzled.*) What a strange looking creature you are, covered with feathers. Shall I cook you like a bird or like a turtle?

NARRATOR: The turtle felt he had really nothing to lose at this point, so he spoke up:

TURTLE: I think I'm better as a turtle. You could pluck off my feathers, and I'll look exactly like a turtle again.

WIFE: Thank you for your suggestion. It's a good idea.

(She starts to remove his feathers.)

You're a very helpful sort of fellow.

NARRATOR: As the feathers were removed, the turtle began to feel like his old self again. This cheered him up a lot, and he began to sing softly. (TURTLE *begins to sing.*) Can you guess what happened this time?

(The WIFE *is taken over by* TURTLE*'s singing which gets louder and louder and she begins to dance.)*

NARRATOR: When the turtle saw what was happening, he sang all the louder. He sang and sang. The farmer returned and said:

FARMER: *(enters followed by* BOY *with corn).* Why, that turtle isn't ready! What is this dancing here? *(He tries to stop his* WIFE, *but he is also overcome by* TURTLE's *singing and joins in dancing, as does the* BOY.*)*

NARRATOR: But the turtle kept on singing, and the farmer and his family danced and danced, and they never even noticed the turtle's friend come in to find him.

PIGEON 1: *(flies on).* Come on quickly. *(Motions to* TURTLE.*)* Follow me. *(Still singing, the* TURTLE *happily scutters off after* PIGEON *who leads him in a little path to exit.)*

NARRATOR: And the turtle sang very loudly and walked very quietly until he was out of sight. *(*FARMER, WIFE *and* BOY *dance off in other direction.)*

FINALE *(optional)*

The Narrator and musicians immediately change the mood with a fast, strong drum beat for the Finale. It can be a short, lively dance with all the performers joining in to make a colorful splash for the closing. If you invite the audience to participate, the dance, of course, will go on much longer and become a party-like celebration!

Pulling It All TOGETHER

1. You are playing the part of one of the characters in "The Turtle Who Wanted to Fly." What will you do to make your character funny?

2. Of all the characters in *Don't Wake the Princess,* which ones did you want to get what they wished for? Why?

3. Tell your own story about a character who has a wish. Compare your story to the stories in *Don't Wake the Princess.*

Books to Enjoy

Stuart Little
by E. B. White
illustrations by
Garth Williams
Born to a human family,
the adventurous young
mouse Stuart Little
searches for his lost
friend, the lovely bird
Margalo.

Robin on His Own
by Johnniece Marshall
Wilson
What Robin *really* wants
is for his mother to come
back. But since that can
never happen, he decides
to do whatever it takes so
that he can stay in the big,
comfortable house where
he grew up.

Bobby Baseball
by Robert Kimmel Smith
Bobby Ellis has no doubts
at all! He just knows he is
going to be a champion
pitcher. Now he has to
prove it to his father—and
to the world.

Julie's Tree
by Mary Calhoun
Julie and her friends
discover that their favorite
climbing tree is to be cut
down to make room for a
parking lot. Can they save
it in time?

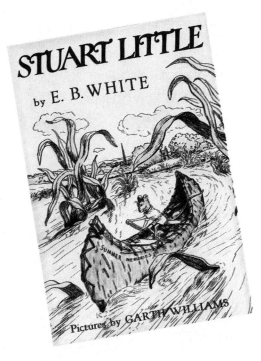

THE GLORIOUS FLIGHT
ACROSS THE CHANNEL WITH LOUIS BLÉRIOT
BY ALICE AND MARTIN PROVENSEN

The Glorious Flight: Across the Channel with Louis Blériot

written and illustrated by Alice and Martin Provensen
Blériot wants to fly more than anything else, and so he begins building flying machines. Will he make it across the English Channel in one of these contraptions?

The Emperor and the Kite

by Jane Yolen
The emperor's daughter is as tiny as can be. When her father is captured, her size doesn't keep her from planning a daring rescue.

Arrow to the Sun

retold and illustrated by Gerald McDermott
In this Pueblo Indian myth, a boy leaves his home on Earth to search for his father, the Lord of the Sun. The pictures are like Indian designs.

Pippi Longstocking

by Astrid Lindgren
Pippi's goal in life is to live exactly as she wishes in her rickety old house with her horse and her monkey, and above all, without any grownups. Would you like to be her neighbor?

Literary Terms

Character

A **character** is a person or animal in a story. Some characters, such as Lentil or the child in *Owl Moon,* are realistic—they seem like people you could really meet. Other characters, Tucker Mouse and Mike's Airedale for example, are fantasy characters.

Fantasy

A story with unreal characters or a setting unlike the real world is a **fantasy.** Some fantasies have animal characters who feel and act just like human beings. These fantasies are called **animal fantasies.** *Tucker Mouse Finds a Friend, The Dog That Pitched a No-Hitter,* and *The Turtle Who Wanted to Fly* are animal fantasies.

Metaphor

A **metaphor** is a comparison between two unlike things. The child in *Owl Moon* says, "But I was a shadow as I walked home." The child was not *really* a shadow, but by comparing herself with one, we learn that the child walked home very quietly.

Plot

The **plot** is the order that things happen in a story. Often the plot develops as the main character tries to solve a problem. For example, Lentil finds a solution to his problem of not being able to sing by learning to play the harmonica so he can make music that way.

Setting

The **setting** of a story is the time and place in which it happens. Sometimes the setting is very important because the story could not take place anywhere else or at any other time. Could *Owl Moon* have taken place anywhere else but in the country at night? Notice that words such as "line of pine trees," and "clearing in the dark woods" are clues that this must be a nighttime country setting.

Simile

An author or a poet may use **simile** to compare two things. A simile usually has the words *like* or *as*. For example, Jane Yolen describes the forest at night as "quiet as a dream."

Glossary

How to use the pronunciation key

After each entry word in this glossary, there is a special spelling, called the **pronunciation**. It shows how to say the word. The word is broken into syllables and then spelled with letters and signs. You can look up these letters and signs in the **pronunciation key** to see what sounds they stand for.

This dark mark (ʹ) is called the **primary accent**. It follows the syllable you say with the most force. This lighter mark (ʹ) is the **secondary accent**. Say the syllable it follows with medium force. Syllables without marks are said with least force.

Vocabulary from your selections

am·bas·sa·dor (am bas′ə dər), a representative of the highest rank sent by one government or ruler to another. *noun.*

an·cient (ān′shənt), **1** belonging to times long past. **2 the ancients,** people who lived long ago. 1 *adjective,* 2 *noun.*

art·ist (är′tist), **1** a person who paints pictures. **2** a person who is skilled in any of the fine arts. **3** a public performer, especially an actor or singer. *noun.*

Az·tec (az′tek), a member of an American Indian people of central Mexico. *noun, plural* **Az·tec** or **Az·tecs.**

cel·e·brate (sel′ə brāt), **1** to observe a special time or day with festive activities. **2** to perform publicly with the proper ceremonies and rites. *verb,* **cel·e·brates, cel·e·brat·ed, cel·e·brat·ing.**

cit·i·zen (sit′ə zən), **1** a person who by birth or choice is a member of a nation: *a U.S. citizen.* **2** an inhabitant of a city or town. *noun.*

clear·ing (klir′ing), an open space of cleared land in a forest. *noun.*

coach (kōch), **1** a large, closed carriage with seats inside and often on top. **2** a person who teaches or trains an athlete or a performer. **3** to train or teach. 1,2 *noun, plural* **coach·es;** 3 *verb.*

coach (definition 2)—a baseball **coach**

com·plain (kəm plān′), to say that something is wrong, troublesome, or painful; find fault. *verb.*

A·140

con·fi·dence (kon/fə dəns), a firm belief in oneself and one's abilities. *noun.*

cot·tage (kot/ij), **1** a small house. **2** a house at a summer resort. *noun.*

de·mon (dē/mən), a devil; evil spirit; fiend. *noun.*

dim (dim), **1** not bright; without much light: *The room is dim.* **2** not seeing, hearing, or understanding clearly. *adjective,* **dim·mer, dim·mest.**

dis·guise (dis gīz/), **1** to make changes in one's clothes or appearance so as to look like someone else. **2** the clothes or actions used to hide or deceive. 1 *verb,* **dis·guis·es, dis·guised, dis·guis·ing;** 2 *noun.*

dis·tract (dis trakt/), to draw away the mind or attention: *The noise distracted me. verb.*

dram·a·tize (dram/ə tīz), **1** to arrange or present in the form of a play. **2** to make seem exciting and thrilling. *verb,* **dram·a·tiz·es, dram·a·tized, dram·a·tiz·ing.**

ech·o (ek/ō), a repeated sound. You hear an echo when a sound you make bounces back from a distant hill or wall so that you hear it again. *noun, plural* **ech·oes.**

em·per·or (em/pər ər), a man who is the ruler of an empire. *noun.*

ESP, See **extrasensory perception.**

a hat	i it	oi oil	ch child	ə stands for:
ā age	ī ice	ou out	ng long	a in about
ä far	o hot	u cup	sh she	e in taken
e let	ō open	u̇ put	th thin	i in pencil
ē equal	ô order	ü rule	ŦH then	o in lemon
ėr term			zh measure	u in circus

ex·tra·sen·sor·y per·cep·tion, understanding or communicating by means other than the five senses. *noun.*

flip·per (flip/ər), **1** one of the broad, flat body parts used for swimming by animals such as seals and walruses. **2** an attachment for the human foot, used as an aid in swimming: *Divers use flippers. noun.*

flipper (definition 1)

gut·ter (gut/ər), a channel or ditch along the side of a street or road to carry off water. *noun.*

har·mon·i·ca (här mon/ə kə), a small musical instrument with metal reeds. *noun.*

her·o (hir/ō), a person admired for bravery, great deeds, or noble qualities. *noun, plural* **her·oes.**

im·age (im′ij), **1** a likeness or copy: *She is the image of her mother.* **2** a picture in the mind. *noun.*

in·dig·nant (in dig′nənt), angry at something unworthy, unfair, or mean. *adjective.*

indignant—She became very **indignant** when she was accused of stealing.

man·ner (man′ər), **1** a way of doing, being done, or happening. **2 manners,** polite ways of behaving. *noun.*

mead·ow (med′ō), a piece of grassy land, especially one used for growing hay or as a pasture for grazing animals. *noun.*

mon·u·ment (mon′yə mənt), something set up to honor a person or an event; anything that keeps alive the memory of a person or an event. *noun.*

molt (mōlt), to shed the feathers, skin, hair, or shell before a new growth. *verb.*

mound (mound), **1** a bank or heap of earth, stones, or other material. **2** the slightly elevated ground from which a baseball pitcher pitches. *noun.*

mur·mur (mėr′mər), **1** a soft, unclear sound that rises and falls a little and goes on without breaks. **2** to make such a soft, unclear sound. 1 *noun,* 2 *verb.*

nib·ble (nib′əl), **1** to eat away with quick small bites, as a rabbit or a mouse does. **2** a nibbling; small bite. 1 *verb,* **nib·bles, nib·bled, nib·bling;** 2 *noun.*

o·rig·i·nal (ə rij′ə nəl), **1** first; earliest. **2** not copied or imitated; new; fresh. **3** a thing from which another is copied, imitated, or translated. 1,2 *adjective,* 3 *noun.*

or·phan (ôr′fən), **1** a child whose parents are dead. **2** to make an orphan of. 1 *noun,* 2 *verb.*

prop·er·ty (prop′ər tē), **1** a thing or things owned; possession or possessions. **2** a piece of land or real estate. *noun, plural* **prop·er·ties.**

puck·er (puk′ər), to draw into wrinkles or folds. *verb.*

ray (rā), **1** a line or beam of light. **2** a line or stream of heat, light, or other radiant energy. *noun.*

ref·uge (ref′yüj), shelter or protection from danger or trouble. *noun.*

A·142

san·i·ta·tion work·er, a person who collects garbage to dispose of. *noun.*

scene (sēn), **1** the time, place, and circumstances of a play or story. **2** a place where something happens or takes place. **3** a view; picture. *noun.*

si·lent (sī′lənt), **1** quiet; still; noiseless: *a silent house.* **2** not speaking; saying little or nothing. *adjective.*

spar·kle (spär′kəl), **1** to send out little sparks. **2** to shine; glitter; flash. **3** a shine; glitter; flash. 1,2 *verb,* **spar·kles, spar·kled, spar·kling;** 3 *noun.*

stare (ster *or* star), to look long and directly with the eyes wide open. A person stares in wonder, surprise, stupidity, curiosity, or from rudeness. *verb,* **stares, stared, star·ing.**

starve (stärv), to suffer or die because of hunger. *verb,* **starves, starved, starv·ing.**

stat·ue (stach′ü), an image of a person or animal carved in stone or wood, cast in bronze, or modeled in clay or wax. *noun.*

a hat	i it	oi oil	ch child	ə stands for:
ā age	ī ice	ou out	ng long	a in about
ä far	o hot	u cup	sh she	e in taken
e let	ō open	u̇ put	th thin	i in pencil
ē equal	ô order	ü rule	ŧH then	o in lemon
ėr term			zh measure	u in circus

stew (stü *or* styü), **1** to cook by slow boiling. **2** food cooked by slow boiling: *beef stew.* 1 *verb,* 2 *noun.*

strat·e·gy (strat′ə jē), the skillful planning and management of anything. *noun, plural* **strat·e·gies.**

stu·di·o (stü′dē ō *or* styü′dē ō), **1** the workroom of a painter, sculptor, photographer, or other artist. **2** a place where motion pictures are made. *noun, plural* **stu·di·os.**

trans·form (tran sfôrm′), to change in condition, nature, or character: *A tadpole becomes transformed into a frog. verb.*

verse (vėrs), **1** poetry; lines of words with a regularly repeated accent and often with rhyme. **2** a single line of poetry. **3** a group of lines of poetry: *Sing the first verse of "America."* *noun.*

war·ri·or (wôr′ē ər), a person experienced in fighting battles. *noun.*

statue—The Statue of Liberty is one of the most famous **statues** in the world.

Acknowledgments

Text

Page 6: *Lentil* by Robert McCloskey. Copyright 1940 by Robert McCloskey, renewed © 1968 by Robert McCloskey. Used by permission of Viking Penguin, a division of Penguin Books USA Inc.

Page 32: "Jacob Lawrence: Painter of the American Scene" by Kathleen Stevens, *Highlights for Children,* Feb. 1989, Vol. 44, No. 2, pp. 16–18. Copyright © 1989 Highlights for Children, Inc. Reprinted by permission.

Page 42: *The River that Gave Gifts,* written and illustrated by Margo Humphrey. Copyright © 1978, 1987 by Children's Book Press. Reprinted by permission of GRM Associates, Inc., Agents for Children's Book Press.

Page 52: "We Could Be Friends" from *The Way Things Are and Other Poems* by Myra Cohn Livingston. Copyright © 1974 by Myra Cohn Livingston. Reprinted by permission of Marian Reiner.

Page 53: "What If" from *The Way I Feel . . . Sometimes* by Beatrice Schenk de Regniers. Text copyright © 1988 by Beatrice Schenk de Regniers. Reprinted by permission of Clarion Books, a Houghton Mifflin Company imprint. All rights reserved.

Page 54: *The Flame of Peace* by Deborah Nourse Lattimore. Copyright © 1987 by Deborah Nourse Lattimore. Reprinted by permission of HarperCollins Publishers.

Page 66: *Owl Moon* by Jane Yolen, illustrated by John Schoenherr. Text copyright © 1987 by Jane Yolen, illustrations copyright © 1987 by John Schoenherr. Reprinted by permission of Philomel Books.

Page 82: "Bird Watcher" from *Bird Watch* by Jane Yolen. Copyright © 1990 by Jane Yolen. Reprinted by permission of Philomel Books.

Page 84: *Sleeping Ugly* by Jane Yolen, illustrated by Diane Stanley. Text copyright © 1981 by Jane Yolen, illustrations copyright © 1981 by Diane Stanley Yennema. Reprinted by permission of Coward, McCann & Geoghegan, Inc.

Page 94: "Why I Wrote *Sleeping Ugly,*" by Jane Yolen. Copyright © by Jane Yolen, 1991.

Page 98: Text and illustrations from *Harry Kitten and Tucker Mouse* by George Selden with illustrations by Garth Williams. Text copyright © 1986 by George Selden. Illustrations copyright © 1986 by Garth Williams. Reprinted by permission of Farrar, Straus and Giroux, Inc.

Page 110: *The Dog That Pitched a No-Hitter* by Matt Christopher, illustrations by Daniel Vasconcellos. Text copyright © 1988 by Matthew F. Christopher. Illustrations copyright © 1988 by Daniel Vasconcellos. Reprinted by permission of Little, Brown and Company.

Page 120: "How I Wrote *The Dog That Pitched a No-Hitter,*" by Matt Christopher. Copyright © by Matt Christopher, 1991.

Page 124: "The Turtle Who Wanted To Fly" from *Plays From African Folktales* by Carol Korty. Copyright © 1969, 1975 Carol Korty. Reprinted by permission of Charles Scribner's Sons, an imprint of Macmillan Publishing Company.

Artists

Illustrations owned and copyrighted by the illustrator.
William Joyce cover, 1, 3–4, 135, 138–139
Robert McCloskey 6–31
Jacob Lawrence 33–34, 39–40
Julie Larkin (calligraphy) 43, 51
Margo Humphrey 42–51
Mary Flock 52–53
Deborah Nourse Lattimore 54–65
John Schoenherr 66–81, 83
Chris Sheban 82–83 (background wash)
Diane Stanley Yennema 84–93, 97
Harry Roolaart 94, 120
Garth Williams 98–109
Daniel Vasconcellos 110–119, 123
Jennifer Hewitson 124–134

Photographs

Page 32: *Builders,* 1980—Jacob Lawrence, Gouache on paper, 34¼ × 25⅜. From the collection of the SAFECO Insurance Companies. Photo: EDEN ARTS/Chris Eden
Page 33: Steven Curtis
Page 34: *Strike,* 1949—Jacob Lawrence. Tempera on hardboard. Permanent Collection, Howard University Gallery of Art, Washington, D.C.
Page 35: EDEN ARTS/Chris Eden
Pages 36–37: *The Migration of the Negro Series,* 1940–41. No. 1: *During the World War There Was a Great Migration North By Southern Negroes*—Jacob Lawrence. Tempera on hardboard, 12 × 18. The Phillips Collection, Washington, D.C.
Page 38: *Harriet Tubman Series,* No. 7, 1939–40—Jacob Lawrence. Casein on hardboard, 17⅛ × 12. Hampton University Museum, Hampton, Virginia
Page 41: *Tools,* 1978—Jacob Lawrence. Gouache on paper, 21¾ × 18½. Collection of Jacob and Gwendolyn Lawrence. Photo: EDEN ARTS/Chris Eden
Page 94: Courtesy of Jane Yolen
Page 120: Courtesy of Matt Christopher
Page 140: SUPERSTOCK
Page 141: Nina Leen
Page 143: Rohan/Tony Stone Worldwide

Glossary

The contents of the glossary have been adapted from *Beginning Dictionary,* Copyright © 1988 Scott, Foresman and Company.